'TIL DEATH:
Marriage Poems

'Til Death: Marriage Poems © 2017 by **Janice Leach & James Frederick Leach**

Published by Raw Dog Screaming Press
Bowie, MD

All rights reserved.

First Edition

Cover illustration: Steven Archer
Book design: Jennifer Barnes

ISBN: 978-1-935738-94-7
Library of Congress Control Number: 2017930025

Printed in the United States of America

www.RawDogScreaming.com

'TIL DEATH:
Marriage Poems

(the horrors & happy afters)

Janice Leach
and
James Frederick Leach

RAW DOG SCREAMING PRESS

Dedicated to all the creative couples who inspire us, including:

Richard Thompson and Linda Thompson,
    especially "Wall of Death"
Patti Smith and Fred Sonic Smith,
    especially "Frederick"
Kim Gordon and Thurston Moore
    especially "The Diamond Sea"
John Doe and Exene Cervenka,
    especially "Fourth of July"
Johnny Cash and June Carter Cash
    especially "Jackson"
Dave Lamb and MorganEve Swain
    especially "Fingers to the Bone"

Helen Nearing and Scott Nearing
Robert Browning and Elizabeth Barrett Browning
Mary Wollstonecraft Shelley and Percy Bysshe Shelley
Jane Kenyon and Donald Hall
Amanda Palmer and Neil Gaiman
Frida Kahlo and Diego Rivera

Art is Hard; Relationships are Impossible
Thanks for showing us how it's done

Table of Contents

I. star-crossed stirrings

Night Course 13
 Shadow of Venus.. 15
stars before the storm 16
The occult encyclopedia
  "Man, Myth & Magic" ©1970
   includes an entry: "Women." 17
Practice 18
This morning 19
Study.. 20

II. dark passions

Serpent Mis-handling.. 22
Beta vulgaris.. 23
Fuckdream #3 24
My favorite square inch 25
Long-Tended Desires 26
Breathe... 27
Lovers of the Silver Age.. 28
Fuckdream #27: Chaperone 29
Dressing Up 30
Fuck Dream #54: Love Nest 31
me, you, here 32
Half Hurt... 33
Spirit Creatures 34
strange ducklings... 35
The Maiden and the Unicorn 36
ending propositions (or, on no one, on down) 39
Float.. 40
The Way We Were 41
Between 42
amazing me 43

Tally 44

III. households

Growing Dust 46
Home Mosaic 47
Garden 48
Companion Planting 49
Through the window, always passing 50
the chatter traps 51
In the Baker's House 52
In My Safe Kitchen 53
Ignition 54
Room for Improvement 55
Remodeling fantasy 56
Opportunity Costs 57
Same Old 58
acceptable substitutions 59
Mending 60
Stitch Fairy 62
black magic 63
Summer Construction 64
Souvenirs 66
What Grows 67
The USS Los Angeles (ZR-3) docks at Lakehurst, NJ 68

IV: spawn/death

Turning of the Year 72
On the turning of the year 74
Finale 76
Broken 77
Pull 78
Lucky Blood 79
Push Yourself 80
dropped stitches 81
Like a Toast 82

basket	84
Standing in the Kitchen, Talking about Danger	85
all yours	86
Agenda	88
Autopsy	89
Nachlass	90
a winter burial	91
Dressed in the Dark	92
Home Movies	93
Ammonite	94
Hunted	95
Second Sight	96
Twice Eurydice	97
The Snow-bike	99
The Ghost Who Didn't Follow Me Home	100
Rocket Man	101
Apocalypse	102
Ostara	104
Samhain	107
Cold Solstice	108

I: star-crossed stirrings

Night Course

I learned our doom early, a lesson poorly heeded.
I was a late 70's teenager, eager for a beard
as heavy and thick as the guitars I adored,
and yearning to pierce my bored suburban sphere,

I took up astrology, the wizard's trivium:
the starry Arithmetic, arcane Design, and mad Poetry of listening
while constellations tell dark knowledge,
any scrap of insight to escape my adolescent crap.

When homework grew tiresome, I plotted latitudes,
reconciled dates, calculated declination,
scanned the crowded columns of tedious ephemerides
to chase the secant of disposition, the cosine of fate.

My pencil would chart this rigid geometry,
scribe precise lines, a criss-crossed sigil
intersecting a circle marked with strange curlicues,
astral characters in trine, square, opposition.

To interpret this potent mandala,
I imagined the namesake gods cavorting,
comporting themselves in similar company,
composing myths to comfort my insignificance.

I met a girl with flowing brown hair,
the scent of her skin its own occult mystery.
We'd dated casually, caressed and kissed,
I cast our fortune and learned the worst.

Her stony goat, sure-footed true would resent

my airy, many-faced flirtations, my quick whimsy.
In time, our relationship would grow to resemble
the grinding erosion of wind against a mountain face.

I took vacation from starry warnings and learned volumes,
spent warm nights reading other signs, pursuing earthy truths,
a summer curriculum in alchemy, in chance and transformation.
That autumn, I closed the heavens' story book for good.

Shadow of Venus

Neither photographer nor astronomer,
I balance musty binoculars, camera phone, sheet of paper
and awkwardly capture the fleeting transit.

I guard my vision, but my photos show a circle, too blurry, too bright
to catch the dark spot I watched—tiny, slowly creeping,
a mote left to imagination, if not record.

The frame omits my spouse who naps inside the yellow room,
my curious streak, my eagerness to fabricate a picture, a poem

some artifact to show him later,
as is my habit, three-decades strong,

the rare and the trivial made solid in the sharing.

stars before the storm

We stretch back side by side under the sudden night sky,
Chins tipped toward the blanket of pinprick lights.
In our own ragged constellation, we observe
The quick movement of the stars of spring.

Through some persuasion, we have altered their orbits.
We managed to pull them along on a Saturday afternoon,
Away from the magnetic draw of friends
To lounge with us in the blackened dome.

Back in the baby days, we might be so configured:
The little boy running from a nightmare or thunder,
The fussy baby nursed into a compliant sleep—
Them against us on any night.

Today in the hushed planetarium with the whirl of projector fans,
they flank us again, like sleepers in a tent,
mouths a-gap. In a row we lean against the upholstery
to watch a perfect miniature sunrise.

The occult encyclopedia "Man, Myth & Magic" ©1970 includes an entry: "Women."

Tie-dyed adolescent of the Aquarian Age
escaping August, its searing boredom,
researched the rare chilled air, the marble library walls,
reviewed the well-thumbed passages
   page 76 of *The Godfather*
   the naked swimmer of *Jaws*...

when, drifting through rows of reference, this series,
its stark black spines embossed with serious, gilt letters,
announced forbidden mysteries, illustrated, exposed.

My parents, protestant, repressed by suburban ignorance,
would discourage these bookish but hormone-fired inquiries,
but I learned every lurid revelation these glossy pages knew,
packed my eyes full of each lascivious truth,
   like the glimpse of sweating flesh
   beneath the scarlet robes of the Baccantes.

Would that I could review these volumes, sprawled privately,
grinding my jeans against bedroom carpet,
invoking their protection against the aches of midnight.
Borrowing this reserved wisdom is forbidden. These secrets must be stolen,
each word swallowed, every image burned, etched in synapse.

Once full, I descended those furrowed, shoe-worn steps, a new initiate
burdened with knowledge, this time-strung fascination, this Magick.

Practice

The first time, there was blood everywhere.
Surrounded by friends in the dark,
the screen filled with shrieking campers meeting the grizzly's frenzy,
he moved in to brush my lips with his.
I felt like cold honey had been poured down my throat.
Something like breathlessness filled my lungs,
but that was just the start.

Behind the octopus arms of grandma's furnace,
behind old curtains transformed to a stage
or a hearth, I tasted the lips of a cousin,
or two. I'd played house with these boys
all my life. Such kisses hardly counted.

A boy from the other side of the other tracks,
who admired my manners,
who took me to one of the highest restaurants
in the city.
Then an heir to the Rothchilds' fortune,
misplaced in the suburbs,
his slow grind against my hip when we made out,
made my stomach cramp.

Warm-up acts for the big top show.
All these years: I'm out of practice.

This morning

This morning,
I woke up before you.
You were golden
in the light from
our curtainless window.
For a long time,
I just watched you breathe.
You looked so young.
I tried to imagine you
when you were the child
I never knew.
All I can be certain of
is that you had blue eyes.

Study

I've made a dig,
uncovered your ruins,
arranged your bones,
named the species.

I've found your tribe,
gone native,
learned your language,
rolled your syllables off my tongue.

I've tugged your wires,
observed your circuitry,
measured voltage,
reseated your connections.

I've cut your skin,
pared back, no secrets,
probed but living,
some holy vivisection.

You needn't fear
my false scholarship.
There's no control in my study,
no conclusions to recommend.

My lack of expertise
exposes my flawed research;
my knowledge's only fund
is my imagination.

II: dark passions

Serpent Mis-handling

> "If it was a snake
> it would have jumped out and bit you."
> —Family Knowledge

Although fang-pricked a thousand times,
this peppered heart doesn't learn, can't detect
the threat; or fear the sudden mouse-trap snap

of a creature grown so common
it coils amid a drawer of balled socks,
curls like foil lurking inside a lunch sack.

Its venom blends like cream in morning coffee,
so obvious, it hides. I limp, wounded
yet oblivious to that jumping, biting love.

Beta vulgaris

When digging hearts, spade carefully
to exhume them whole, unbloodied.
Brush away their dirt,
caress them in warm water.

A sharp knife and surgical precision
—aim an inch above the aortic crown—
avoids carnage, the permanent stain.
A clean bisection yields two treats:

I choose the tender leaves
sautéed with a vinegar spritz.
My lover prefers the red flesh.
For him, I simmer these hidden meats,

until their thick skins relax, loosen.
When cool, I undress them by hand
grab—squeeze
until the taproot slips out naked.

He devours them, these ruby organs,
sinking teeth into gore-colored fruits.
This tonic wakes the blood.
My reward: a kiss from his red, red lips.

Fuckdream #3

Worn raw, genitals aglow, spent,
muscles weary, radiant, we rest.
Hearts, those fluttering doves, nest
and consciousness quivers, winks away.

Our present languor changes, an ancient site.
Frame and mattress become splinters, dust.
And us? A couple of skulls, a filigree of mingled ribs
collapsed upon the fragile coils of vertebrae.

Ezekiel straddles our conjoined skeletons,
curses, winding flesh upon the loom of our bones,
knitting skin around our mismatched remains.
He rushes. Gabriel's horn is urgent, impatient.

With our cobbled imperfect resurrection-corpses complete,
we rise, stagger, one flesh married again.

My favorite square inch

If I praise too loudly
Of your middle-aging flesh,
You blush and fuss and dart away
Or doubt my words' intent.

To celebrate you whole
Seems too large, too generous?
Then I will focus my gaze
On my favorite small spaces:

That valley where hip, stomach, and thigh meet,
the delicate indent of skin;
An intersection invites my ear
To hear the rushed blood river move within.

The center of your back, where your halves divide
the hard, flat space above the round;
I rest my head while you read
On a trail of fine hairs.

Behind your ear, the junction
Where skin blends into scalp;
A place you cannot see, but sense,
The edge my lips trace and press.

And the blue center of your eye.
I settle not on just a parcel,
But declare this landscape home,
Lay claim to every inch of your terrain.

Long-Tended Desires

The blood of a sapling, green, coursing just beneath a husk of bark erupts,
an amber teardrop, gleaming, squeezed to clear expression
submerges, a spring limb ready to bend and bend again;

A heavy pitcher lashed to sinews along the back, the shoulders.
Its awkward tug against the legs, so eager to spill its precious burden,
to drown your hidden roots, to anoint your tender stalks;

a fist of hard tendrils, knotted to the bony fingers of a trellis,
the promise of fruit, long ago impertinent
to this constant struggle of strut anchored in a deep vein, of branch
   wrapped tight, relentless.

Breathe

I've been doing this for years,
listening to you breathe,
it's become like my own breath,
something I don't hear unless it's different.

You are not my second self
nor my mirror, but in this river
you are the water
next to my moving current.

Along the shallows, twisting the bends
both under and over,
impossible to separate one wave
from the next.

Lovers of the Silver Age

Is anything so ugly
as a fat man crying,
his bulbous middle
rippling in grief?

The crown of gilded cardboard
tilts low on his knobby brow.
Lament can merely dislodge,
not remove, its mocking honor.

His dwelling grand cathedral
is exile from true sanctuary.
It knows so little peace,
a gargoyle's stony vigil.

He'd devour his own head
served on a filthy platter,
if this meal arrived
during one of his moods.

The molten chime of metal bells
pouring from steeples, the peeling eaves,
release retribution like prison rain.
His wasted dreams of Esmeralda,

that heroic dancer in the square
escapes in a horse drawn cart,
while amid the pious ramparts,
a squatting Quasimodo weeps.

Fuckdream #27: Chaperone

I promenade my pale lover through the nervous crowd
of waifs in evening gowns, beanpole tuxedos, their hands like anxious birds.
We chuckle, so comfortable in our memories, in our present station.

Your trembling arm wraps my waist, a pose of perfect affection
'til the balance tips and you lean fully against me
collapsing as I scoop you into my embrace, romantic but troubled.

Your skin is so loose around your frame of bones.
Your nipple slips out, shifts to rest like a wart on your shoulder.
I tuck it underneath your shawl, embarrassed, terrified.

You continue to shrink in my arms, deflate, whisper with effort,
"The hospital keeps a mixture of my vital fluids."
The music, a piercing crescendo. The lights, gone. All gone.

Dressing Up

My furry chin informs me
of my recent lapse, my werewolf form,
endured in rage
for just under a month,

long enough for stubble
to curl into whiskers
to blur side burns,
smear the mustache.

Today I draw a razor line
through obscure foam,
scrape a face, a sketch,
pretend it's smooth again.

This morning my human mask
nearly fits as awkward as
a hermit crab scuttling
into its borrowed shell.

Fuck Dream #54: Love Nest

The courtyard was a mess of gems
of broken glass, tiny can-shaped capacitors.
I'd quit the day before, made good on my promise,
and tradition held that any technician
could smash the last machine he worked on
for closure, vengeance for pointless toil.

We were finally young and free, your breasts firm and high.
I unbuttoned your flannel shirt just inside the swinging doors.
Shameless in our leisure—no jobs on a workday morning,
we haunted the barn, the post-industrial bunk-house
scoping locations to fuck and sleep and stir our mischief.

You folded black paper airplanes to fly reconnaissance.
The attic was mounded with hay, pierced with great windows.
A massive engine clackered in the corner, spewing gravity.
Our desire was congenial, adapted to circumstance.
We settled against the cool cement, the public hallway.
You curled backward, complicit with my body's wishes.

The ground gave way, a slow crumble
to an underworld of dusty scraps, slanted sun beams.
A perfect nest til our amours disturbed a vicious mother possum
and her half-formed litter, larva with pale fur, those maggot-mammals.
She charged, her triangular snout valiant with teeth
snapped to the bridge of my nose. Her jaw shook my skull,
finally rattling my bones loose from sleep, lost to love.

me, you, here

The me who doesn't like you doesn't tolerate fools,
doesn't appreciate sincere incompetence or silly good will.
That me is dis-satisfied with cow-eyed, stupid purity, doesn't cherish
our stale precious history. *This* me, doesn't love.

You woo the worst of me, savor choice delicacy
the gristled valves of my calloused heart, plate up
the leather flaps hidden amid my private tissues,
my innards most inedible. You treat an autopsy as buffet.

My whole expanse is yours, a deed sealed and signed,
yet some is posted land, where irregular geysers spew,
where rocky crusts scarcely conceal a chemical Hell.
All things are permitted, some do not edify.

Trust your nose, love, before you devour the meal;
When you chance on some caustic cavern pool, don't bathe.

Half Hurt

Swallow marbles
one by one
cold glass
throat slide
final belly plunk
the cool tick
of counted pennies
dropping in a pile:
it adds up.

Crawl over rough wood
prick of uneven grain
scratch of splinter
festers under skin
the ache and worry
flesh-cocooned sliver
tissue swaddled.

We share hurts
like the shard of a tooth
sunk deep in soft matter
spar or tournament
feign or truth:
if I hurt you half as much
as you hurt me,
I don't know how you live.

Spirit Creatures

In the tree outside the bedroom window,
Raccoons fight or fuck—
Who knows—it sounds the same.

We channel them as we lean in
to worship or whack,
a growl we recognize as our own.

This love's teeth will not let go,
fierce, like a bite or a scratch or a claw,
that kills or saves again.

strange ducklings

We awake in flight, mid-migration,
feather-tips intertwined, wing to wing,
mated for life, fated for the honk
of black beaks on graceful white arcs.

Not quite the grail-cursed Lohengrin;
far from the god-raped Leda.
In our dreams, this dalliance is scored
by Saint-Saens, voiced by Casals,

like my dad's scratchy '78, the thick platter,
wobbling hypnotically on the turntable,
like water coursing in a dark stream.
The round pond of destiny. Endless.

How long have we flown, slumbering?
Dare we wake and risk a crash like Icarus?

The Maiden and the Unicorn

I

    In Capital City, girls need gold to live
    And Mammon is the one to know for gold.
    A warmly-tempered man, he can relieve
    The chill from maiden breasts whose blood's run cold.
    Repaying this in kind, Mammon's fold
    Of fillies keeps the local plowboys warm.
    He also deals virility, sold
    In these phylacteries of powered horn
Whole rumored origin is the mythic unicorn.

    A maiden came today from Meadow-wood.
    She wore her widest smile and whitest dress
    She hoped he looking like a winged joy would
    Help her looking for employers to impress.
    Her plans instead prepared distress;
    She raised a mean commotion at Mammon's Machine
    Where workers stared, which made her count success,
    At her awesome oddness, like virgin cattle's cream,
Or snow unfallen of which the clouds themselves dream.

    Abruptly, Mammon spoke and broke her spell:
    "A little thin, at least she's budded at the breast.
    "Virgin?" Yes, her blush attested well.
    "Untried! If you need work, I need a test
    "To prove you can preform what maids do best:
    "Take this saw and with it hack the growth
    "From off the crown of that proud forest-pest,
    "The Unicorn. His waste of that resource I loathe.
Return the horn and harvest wage and reward both."

'Til Death

II
>	Her rumpled gown and all are sprawled on this glade.
>	She cries and tries to dream her errand ends
>	In daily wages, gladly made and paid—
>	And not in false betrayal of her childhood friend,
>	The Unicorn, her shining knight they would pretend,
>	Whose sword of Light dispelled her darkest fears.
>	Alas, He likes his ladies chaste and defends
>	That virtue 'gainst a goblin troop of leers.
> Her current dream deserves his sneers, and hence, her tears.

>	Nearby, the mystic equine echoes his mistress,
>	Pawing the earth that beneath him his tears soak:
>	"The horn forbids my crown to wear a harness
>	With yonder team. 'No work, no worth,' they joke."
>	The maiden, cheered, reveals what Mammon spoke
>	Which fills them both with dreams of daily bread.
>	So they sacrifice the horn with gleeful strokes.
>	On the lap where the creature reuses his beastly head,
> The horn, once sawn, spills blood and stains the gown red.

>	As no Delilah calls her Sampson "fool,"
>	Neither does the Maid cry "simpleton!"
>	They part the best of friends. The Golden Rule
>	Intact, since onto each their will was done.
>	From childish magic trees both children run
>	To Field and City and their adult profession:
>	To learn themselves why men call Mammon "demon"
>	And "hell" the place you work and labor "sin"
> And cool pursuits of cash, a "chasing after wind."

III
>	Grown to woman now, she wears that gown,
>	Its stains unfaded still, and not concealed
>	But flaunted on the streets she paces down.

Leach

Her hero reigns, no doubt, some nearby field
A proof, himself of alchemy revealed,
Who, beast of burden once, now owns the team.
Their separation soon will be repealed.
So, fed too well on discontent and dreams
She strayed today from Mammon's flock for pastures green.

With every forward step, her faith is halved:
"Could he remain unchanged, though shorn?" she doubts.
With formulated proverbs, her faith is salved:
"A magic beast, if truly blest, would spout
More horns 'til seven times seven all fall out!"
Yet since no Beast, if male, transcends deceit,
She plans to smooth her hands along his snout
(A subtle female ploy to check his teeth)
And chest (to see if Trojan rhythms beat beneath.)

She finds him, his strength like knotted leather thongs
Wrapped to a wagon dragged through the sand, and forgets
Her doubt: "Unicorn, our home is among
"The Honey Mountains, where bread undrenched in sweat
"Is sweet. Our virgin dreams are valid yet."
And even then she knew his answer, before
He drooled those loud, cold words that dripped regret:
"Mere dreams cannot redeem us anymore
"For I am now a worn-out horse, and you, a whore."

ending propositions
(or, on no one, on down)

When I buried you last night
    your blue toes stuck out
    of the oddly formed coffin.
Those swollen feet I made sure not to puncture
As I screwed the inadequate cover down.

I was quite insane since you left me for dead.
    I slowly piled the soil up.
    It ran in through the makeshift lid.

I did not see your face again.
    How could I, having postponed
    your internment for so long?

You took a day and a half to die.
    Why did I take so much longer
    just to say goodbye?

Someone will tear down this hill,
    check my grim handiwork,
    learn how poorly I made your bed,
And I shall wear my guilt like a suffocating darkness,
a restless mourning shawl.

Float

no tether snap, no rocket crash
no tragic launch or fatal landing
left us drifting, listless, lost

like cosmonauts whose nation vanished
its gravity suspended, gone
once their craft achieved its orbit.

With no command to call us home
or terminate our mission, we wait
and wheeze the air of decadence,

eat our meals—recycled shit—
and risk of this weightless dance with God
encased in endless hollow peace.

The Way We Were

You wore pumps and gray flannel to the noir betrayal
where you agreed to Robert Mitchum's demands.
He poured two fingers neat from the bottom drawer bottle,
You swallowed hard, demanded more, then agreed

to ruin my dreams. Deep undercover, shrouded
in suburban drapes, buried with two car mortgages
kid's dentists career… You'd coax me by degrees
to surrender to boredom's sweet release, ennui.

"You ain't souring the pickle-barrel, sweetheart,"
that gray-scale dick explained. "He's a hack. A schlub."
In wordless response, you pursed your black lipstick,
dark kisses punctuating a face without affect. Judas.

In this dream you smoke a cruel cigarette.
I shouldn't have fallen for Lauren Bacall.

Between

Between sheets and sunrise,
I curl cat-like around
the spot where you should be,
where only a cool shadow
lies on your pillow, refusing
to warm. I wait there for dreams
to wrap up my loneliness, to steal away
and leave me to anticipate
our exhaustive comprehension.
The best of me awaits
your gentle uncovering.

amazing me

Astonishingly, you mystify me still:
How can your body, known better than the road home,
provide adventurous surface for my hands?
Why can your gentle brush down my hair
tighten my stomach like a first kiss?

Tally

It's no competition, these **body sports**
these unscheduled bouts, the **regular** escapades,
tournament, accounting

We don't keep score–though she'd be winning
her triple play–a crackle, a **blaze**, a grand firework–
to his every geyser blast.

lazy, glazed in sweat we **ponder**
our career statistics, from **rookie** season
all warmup.

the fantasy teams enlisted

completed.

in this never-ending exhibition,
everyone wins. Prizes for **all**.

III: house holds

Growing Dust

The woman who lived in my house
before me never bothered
to dust the tops of doors
or window sills, never
scrubbed under her stove,
never noticed, I suppose,
the dust and the dirt.
When I moved in,
I noticed rubber bands, marbles,
cat food stuck in the floor vents.
I scrubbed,
dusted, and bothered.

But she planted the flowers
along the side of the house,
by the front porch, in the backyard.
That first spring, they took me
by surprise as I shook
out a rug on the front steps.
They must have been there before
preparing to bud even without me
noticing or bothering with them.
No violets, my favorite, or marigolds.
And the rows weren't straight.
Present as they were, I let them be.

Home Mosaic

Our modest house, a whole century
old, was built for simple folks like us.
My partner and I remember them each spring
when the garden earth yields of their secrets:

the chips of dropped cups, the crumbs of china;
the jagged necks of bottle glass,
some root beer brown, some a pale kaleidoscope,
a jigsaw treasure we piece into tales while we till.

I posit a bachelor, a bit distracted,
embarrassed by decades of drunken clumsiness
or laudanum tremors. He buried the evidence
near his roses and professed innocence.

My love imagines a couple. One ordinary evening,
as a last dish dripped on the rack,
the woman considered her mate, his cigar, its ash…
and she smashed her entire cupboard bare.

Her anger abated, unquenched. She stood to her ankles
in shards of keepsakes and marriage gifts.
Her husband, composure shattered, entered ranting.
She briskly swept her kitchen, her life, clean.

The story astonishes the trowel from my glove.
I stammer, "Why did she wash the dishes first?"
My enigmatic partner responds a gleaming smile,
porcelain, implacable, precious.

Garden

You're a garden, all poison thorns,
prickle weeds, hidden toads.
No Eden, few Earthly Delights.
A waste overgrown, luscious and resplendent.

Even knowing this evil nature, its rotting heart,
your stony paths entice me,
lure me toward shaded groves of noxious foliage,
where tangled recesses strangle the sun.

The cool soils of your beckoning beds,
the invitations of your invasive tendrils,
the call of your wilds, your caresses
entwine my limbs, link my veins, sap my pulse.

Root through my inner rooms, my black matter,
and I become loam; you, my final plot.

Companion Planting

When the soil's warmed,
we tuck the seeds in the shallow dark,
deciding placement by compatibility.
We think a plant needs neighbors,
requires company perhaps,
to share the dirt and space.
Unseen encouragements
might be exchanged while
sympathetic worms
loosen the earth,
allow roots to spread.
Foliage stretch and reach
might work together
to shade the interstitial dirt
and block the competition.
Basil and tomatoes
make good companions;
fennel has few friends.
A gardener's myth
tells us plants support
each other in growing and thriving,
more philosophy than science,
not unlike true love.

Through the window, always passing

With my hands in dish water
or drawing a knife through onion half on the wooden board,
my attention tugged away too late
to catch a clear view.
A shift of shadow
or shadow of shadow.
At twilight
or when the sun slants under the curtain,
I glimpse perhaps a wrinkled sunbeam,
spying movement, not substance;
I'm no true witness,
but I've seen them
through the window, always passing.
Former neighbors or inhabitants
lingering still outside.
Their almost movements
make me turn again
toward the chill breath
trace of dust in the air.
I see they were there,
when they are gone.

the chatter traps

Almost ghosts, the squirrels return this autumn
to haunt our eaves and the crevices the idiot builder
left for them. These yearly children do not listen
To reason. They require violent exorcism.

They chatter us awake, we late morning sleepers.
The drywall above our double bed is cracked
at the edges where I batter my fists blue to quiet them,
where I rattle the joists they gnaw to loosen their teeth.

Last year, one burrowed through the walls, caught itself
between our room and where my two-year old sleeps.
I called its desperate scratching at the plaster
just a lonely teddy bear who wants a hug goodnight.

I shot that creature a month later as it poked through
the kitchen's cracked ceiling. "Rats with tails" my neighbor
called them, when I return the weapon.
My fingers trembled from the discharge, my first kill.

This year, I opt for traps, ones to let these unwanted entities live.
And vow to release them to infest some distant cemetery.
I place the cages in the animal darkness, the recesses of our home
foredoomed as shelters, reaching where I cannot see.

Leach

In the Baker's House

In the baker's house,
mistakes become dinner,
flaws become dessert.
The grit of flour
settles like dust.
In the baker's house,
yeast is a god,
sugar is life,
and icing and butter
flow like rivers.
In the baker's house,
honey and cinnamon
stick to the surfaces,
spice the skin
with joy and appetite.
In the baker's house,
waste is a sin,
burnt is sacrilege,
bread is a sacrament
sliced up and shared.

In My Safe Kitchen

In my safe kitchen
where cups seldom fly against walls,
we drink tea in smooth blue mugs.
Coming off the evening shift,
Mary talks of quiet
at the crisis center—broken
by the entrance of a woman,
needing kleenex and ice.
Mary made the call, trying not
to look, eyes shut against her will.

Like paperwork, the cops arrive
with blanks to fill.
She tells me now, stirring her tea,
how the cop had to bite
his lip, to turn away.
She tells me "She was so small.
How could anyone do that?"
I turn to make more tea,
holding down the mugs.

Ignition

Maybe it won't be
global warming, peer pressure,
heart disease, petty squabbling,
inflation, the 7 year itch—times 4—,
apnea, vitamin deficiency,
evolution, peri-fucking-menopause,
national debt, spiritual warfare,
middle-age spread, slowing metabolism,
nerves, high blood pressure,
back taxes, radon,
hypocrisy, or forgetting to floss
that will do us in.

Perhaps our worries issue
from the contemplative breath
of the enameled, brooding, chrome-trimmed
kitchen Buddha, our ancient stove—
erratic, antique, conspiring, silent—
its slow invisible exhale,
its cough the spark of the end.

Room for Improvement

My sander whines, nags as I drag it along. Hers too. Worse,
if our tools were silent, we too would yell, squeal, screech,
ineffectively, but necessary at this stage in the process, in the frustration.
We compressed our overstuffed lives, again made space for this work.

So, near yet not close, we labor, isolated by noise, ears corked with foam.
Mask the curses we mutter under our choked breath.
Back and forth, the repetitions numb our muscles, our minds.
But just now, I gaze across the small room at you, hunched, aching.

We've already torn away the ragged carpet, wrenched up
the strips of vicious nails, pried out the stray staples
and now we grind away layers, starting coarsely,
a ruthlessness perversely therapeutic.

With each pass we regain tenderness, erase the earlier scratches,
until, despite the dirt, the warps, the splinters, patches of beauty emerge,
the undulating grain dancing down the planks of ancient pine,
its resinous dust tasting like Christmas trees, like history well spent.

But nothing is finished yet. We still might triumph
or just muddle through to completion
or abandon everything undone—so many others do.
What fools entrust such precious tasks to amateurs?

Remodeling fantasy

Later you can say
to your second wife,
the one who comes after
the first one wears out,
that you never liked that color,
that it wasn't your idea,
that the tile was so crooked you can
hardly crap straight.

But for now,
let's just say,
"Good job."

Opportunity Costs

Roof in our bellies;
four square meals
holding off the ravages
of a wild heaven.

Cyclone fencing
to keep out the chill;
occasional clothing
for masquerade smiles.

Astride two worlds,
bohemian, suburban,
inspired, respectable,
torn from crotch to crown.

When put like that, our bounty
is well worth the squandered time.

Same Old

The same old fight is dull.
It's drilling teeth,
washing walls,
the same old words
used as swords,
cutting flesh or souls,
deep knife wounds
festering, burning,
bleeding the usual way.

The same old sex is not.
It's a fresh snack,
a surprise ingredient,
discovering a hidden room, the secret door
where all the treasures are kept,
a sparking fire,
golden, unruly, tender.
Knowledge that burns
the usual way.

acceptable substitutions

We were out of cream,
so I pissed in your cup,
out of eggs so I served
scrambled turds with cracked pepper.
You complimented my ingenuity.

You, lost in constant worries,
burned the bills, the paycheck,
the junk mail, deposited
the ashes in the bank. The teller
marked the contribution in charcoal.

Too tired to fuck,
we fought instead,
all night long, our knives
slicing the sheets,
shredding the mattress.

Mending

Before this morning's church, I watched my Jim
struggle into his resale shop jacket;
his shirt sleeve caught the lining, which
threatened to slide down and out with his hand.

While our baby sleeps, the lamp
casts reading light over shoulders,
illuminates my sewing box, a rainbow
of cylinders beside the grey coat.

A single evergreen strand
passes with camel-like resistance
through the narrow eye
mirroring a squinting slant.

Thread wraps my finger, rolls off my thumb.
I pinch tight and tug to form a knot.
For inside repair no one will see,
this eye chose forest green.

I smooth the lining flat
against the facing, opening it
like a child untwists a morning glory,
gathering a clue of how its made.

Someone has been here before
and left her traces of matched thread to mend
the damage of too much fondness. Her skill
passed inspection when I smoothed the collar.

Missing stitches leave a memory of crisp holes
that line the cloth like paws on snow. I follow
her tracks over the shoulder, under the arm,
stepping to re-trace her design.

Some places where I put stitches
they have not been for years; some places
I sew right over her threads, pulling taut
this link until our colors blend.

Stitch Fairy

You knit a bit.
You dropped a stitch.
You tossed the work.
You asked me to fix.

I picked up your work.
I counted rows.
I worked the yarn.
I mended holes.

I tell my friend
Your knitting woes:
That I fixed up skips
And lined up rows.

Was he asleep?
She asked of me.
When you played
magic yarn fairy?

I had to laugh.
That's not our guise.
We're twisted threads
not tangled lies.

black magic

the dirty clothes cauldron overflows
its foul brew and fills our small apartment's
floor with clots of socks, darkened undergarments,
a grayish broth and steam. —Our discarded clothes

had grown among us, a forest of fungus clumps.
I dared to gather these rank ingredients
and stew the crease charm that conjures compliments.
My crowded washer churns a curse instead and dumps

its soapy load of dreams: my mom's machine,
a heart enlarged by love, allowed
entire closets, emptied drawers, and I, somehow,
could climb inside, and congregate among the clean.

—and so, ankle deep in evil suds,
I know:
    I'm not the man my mother was.

Summer Construction

A year that pallet sat, stacked full
with timbers left from last year's porch.

All winter I watched, chewed cigar ends,
as weather bent my wood, twisted it
like headless flower stems, turning
perhaps according to the world's curve.

'Til now I stood by, when under
later summer's humid dark green
I sort the lumber across the lawn
attempting to make the most of what I may.

My neighbor bets its only fit for (building) fires
which makes my ox-head more determined:
The fragments will wreathe my sagging wisteria.
I'd seen such a trellis during my spring travels.

Since the beginning, the wood resists my tidy design.
No four odd pieces form an even square.
Even as my clever joinery coaxes a straighter joint
my thick (common) nails spilt the sticks to kindling.

And so I curse the wood (occasionally) with reason:
"These seem truly damned materials, Lord.
Expect just so much redemption, even from
Your own workman." So I swear, but work on.

Finally I prop the cage against the porch to admire
no uniform construction, ignoring their ragged posture,
yet content that the Creator finds very good
what we mortals can accomplish with such warped wood.

Souvenirs

In each dusty shop, boutique, thrift store,
I look for you, for your likeness,
in objects to fly back to you.
Like a magpie with my trinkets,
I'll lay them at your feet like myrrh and gold.
If I could find that relic, that place holder,
an invisible paperweight to store in your pocket,
lucky as a penny, polished smooth with value,
then I could place a lien against your heart.
I've studied you like archeology,
uncovered your ruins, arranged your bones;
I know you are my tribe,
something no one else has, just mine.
I know when I see it, like a tune
that I've forgotten:
some magic knowledge
will place it in my hand.
All at once familiar,
a story unfolding like an origami bird,
each crease a memory
that now belongs to you.

What Grows

From the window above, through the frost-etched glass,
the ground wavers under our touch. Once on the shortest day of the year,
Jim measured and marched a circle and placed bricks to mark
the round bed. Now the rectangles nudge up, budding through the snow
like early crocuses or a Stonehenge.

Year-round, the garden grows, soil freezing and thawing, surfacing
the lost and planted remnants of its former tenants.
The same shovel that's five times
turned that soil finds a file rasping on the metal.

Each rock moved shifts the balance, anthill pushed aside,
and ground shifts back, giving a hollyhock, a pumpkin, a moonflower
we didn't ask for. We uncover something new for every bit we bury.

Each element has its season: plant or bug or weed. A good year for tomatoes,
a good one for flea beetles—no telling what will thrive.
Asparagus beetles almost finished off their host the first year—
fronds stripped to branches by the little worms,
their squished innards revealed the exact color of the plants.

Our old house grows out of old soil. We don't know how many
hands have tilled this dirt, called this patch a garden. Like them,
we take credit for the dirt, as we take credit for us. We think
because we plant it, it will grow, that we make something as primordial
as love. We fail seasonally, but try again to please the earth
with our offerings, try to win its love.
Always, forgiveness sticks to us like dirt.

The USS Los Angeles (ZR-3) docks at Lakehurst, NJ

An obscene panorama
Hangs above our headboard
The pallet where we stage
Our own private docking.

A dirigible, its turgid skin
all silver-gray, paper-beige—
Slowly noses toward
a lascivious cavern
The ample barn, able to house
Its full girth and length.

Foreplay has settled to serious work.
Door flung wide, hungry, eager.
The airship forsakes its wind-riding display
but the show is not entirely finished.

Observers, tiny as dots, watch
as these pornographic dinosaurs
ease themselves together, an act
of massive, erotic majesty.

We, watchers too, re-enact this ritual
As often as befits our mortal
our windowed timbers. Our integument,
hydrogen-engorged.

'Til Death

Ancients recognized such shameless displays
celebrated similar passions with
a quatrain or couplet or even a primal image,
encoded naughty wisdom.

Two dragons exhausted from battle
One yawns to swallow the other, whole.
One opening, one tail: One flesh.
Ourorboros.

IV: spawn/death

Turning of the Year

faith

1
These times will not return to us; no simple turn
of cycles wheels around again, nor even measures,
our precious and specific treasures: like William's birth,
his wail, his crap, his anxious crawl to early steps—
or marriage vows or slow embraces while we dance—
If Time is just a wheel, it cannot be that round.

2
And Time is not a line or simple curve if round;
Two points cannot describe how loving moments turn
to anger; nor formulas how wrestles chance to dance.
What is it, then, that the calendar measures,
if not itself? Since time proceeds like baby steps:
enthusiasm tumbling limbs forward from birth.

3
From head to toe, Time itself resembles birth:
—Its living fullness presses flesh firm and round,
—(Its blessed beasts impend despite our cautious steps!)
—It reaches deep inside us, helping the fetus turn,
—Its labor isn't toil nor meaningless, the measure
taken assisting: its end redeems the frantic dance.

4
And with its end obscured, Time becomes a dance
performed by movements, both minute and grand, both birth
and bread, by those who can't compose its rhythms measures,
nor decide that its geometry is round.

Despite ourselves, we wholly choose to take our turn
and stumble down the floor, propelled by rustic steps.

5
Creation can't progress, except with waltzing steps.
Its forward-two to backward-one admits the Dance
can draw those mystic lines, that mothers claim can turn
a simple kiss into the pretext for a birth.
It does! Since William, now our family circles round,
Dizzy speculation what the term "tomorrow" measures.

6
Only the Music is contact: its ceaselessly coursing measures
Rise as holy incense does from temple steps.
Alone, its logos brings our dancing circles round,
A Christ whose blood redeems our dismal march to dance.
And so our years revolve around our savior's Birth,
The One 'round who the cosmos also makes their turn.

7
(A metaphor that measures Time will always turn
awry: its slippery steps will blur the figure's birth.
Imagine the atoms in round quantums. Describe their dance!)

On the turning of the year

death

25
Soon this year will end; the calendar will turn
to paper scraps where once we scrawled our months' slow passing.
And worse, the change presents no salve for doubt;
We cannot praise the solstices as holy points,
since Spring itself brings no salvation, only April's march
to June and onward still, onward without end.

26
Despite the endless trek, we cannot choose our end.
The narrow, straight parades we sketch will often turn
without consent and play an unfamiliar march.
Alone, we walk and think we own our lives, while passing
no intended destination, now even points
of reference. Ahead, our future clouds in doubt.

27
But even though it is obscured, we cannot doubt
our lives will end. And at that unexpected end
will be a cross, with wooden arms aflame, which points
to hell and home. And with its fire some beasts will turn
to reformed creatures; others only melt while passing,
to joyless alloy, or harden to statues where they march.

28

But knowing this does not resolve our daily march.
"All is nought" is no solution, nor is doubt

that even in the transient beauty of creation passing,
there is meaning; even after mortal glories end.
We must find better recourse than to pace and turn
our heads to face the ground, ignoring all the glorious points.

29
Others posit "progress" as if creation points
itself toward a heaven, to which we uphill march:
"As planets revolve, we beasts evolve and turn
to better beasts, replacing love for hate and doubt
And every action on its own will bring this end."
Alas, no actor acts alone and purity too is passing.

30
If years revolve, then all these moments, passing
on the broken wheel, are equidistant points;
We are no nearer center than to journey's end
Their cyclic harvest threshes souls for death's cold march,
while its mesmerizing spin sows seeds of doubt:
"Could Christ be just the hub of this huge circle's turn?"

31
What vision are we passing on of Time: to turn
the faithless home with points that double their surest doubt
in how the world will end? Marking Time, we march.

Finale

I've been awake those hours,
early, just after the first blush.
I've made coffee and walked
this baby over the broken
kitchen tiles, over hand-covered elbows
clasped around her knees to lock my arms.
Though I never write a word
before breakfast, I understand
this summer, the weary sunrise,
the final poem, the surrender—
and I never did before.

Broken

If we emerge in ten-toed perfection,
we do not stay that way.
Some discover early
what we all find out eventually:
we cannot count on these shells.

A series of stubs and snags await:
sharp edges, spinning tires, weak valves,
hole in the heart,
our flaws uncovered.

And what happens to us:
What gets done in the dark,
or in the crowd, accidents, falls,
too much, not enough.

The days are hard on us all.
I want to assure you:
you are no more broken than the rest.
That love doesn't fix anything really,
but what other tools do we have?

Pull

In the blue light of morning, in snow muffled treads,
Orange glow whispers along, one step behind the shadows,
Warm fingers working up the back of the earth.
The sun's made a seductive loop, moving closer,
And yet the earth resists, coldly shifts a shoulder
And pulls away. Later, earth blossoms, showy
And green, turning a luxuriant smile sunward,
And both feel the tug.
Circling, hovering, orbiting, they play out
Their ridiculous attraction, not getting any closer.
We smile, amused, still drawn.
It is, after all, the only arrangement we know.

Lucky Blood

Alone, it seemed, she generated a family. Ten children
and no father-presence. It's said she ruled
with a switch or a hairbrush, underlining her reign
with a welt, if need be.

A poor woman's death requires no will,
and she left none. No goods but these:
dream books, lists of friends from childhood,
pictures some labeled with the names
written across the chests of Ova, Alma, Shirley,
lists of birthdates, addresses lived,
calendars as chronicles.

What made her two-room,
carpeted, balconied, air-conditioned
apartment the best place
she'd ever lived?
       The past.

Enough to eat, to play
the lottery, to afford the luxury of
embroidering time gone by
—that was wealth.

Push Yourself

Last autumn, we made the trip to the farm
like it was no big deal. We arrived to find
dinner had become a big top event.
There, like a wheel-chair Barbara Walters,
she grilled all the cousins and children
on their lives and other current events.

After hot dogs and pies, three small cousins led Jim and I
through the corn maze their father had cut,
and we followed, being baffled and encouraging
and adventurous under the warm September sun.
When we tired of being lost, we followed the barn roof
to the exit, appearing between stalks like magical travelers.

Driving home, we stopped for a coffee
and a tablet of morphine to smooth the road.
Later we would talk about that perfect day.
Later I would recall how she'd often say she had to push
herself or she'd never get anything done.
We didn't miss that show. We'd all pushed.

dropped stitches

Little survives; nothing I've made
with needle and knotted yarn.

The cancer scarf for Mom
its tight rows of regal purple
flecked with red and blue,
a wrap for her chemically frail shoulders,
a hug when I was gone to work.
She misplaced it at physical therapy
then cursed herself to the grave.

She lost her hair, that carrot mop,
so I attempted a cap, but that impossible spiral
of five choreographed needles
frustrated my restless, clumsy fingers
until they snapped the sticks,
wadded the yarn, buried all in the trash.

Mother had slipped into that near-death, that final sleep,
when an old friend arrived from out of state
to deliver a prayer shawl. She stood bedside,
raised hands over mother's unconscious form,
muttered quiet words, a private benediction
Mother never woke to feel.

Some eternal thrift shop, some bureau
of lost and found, perhaps collects
these dropped stitches, these forgotten garments.
Perhaps. I know, at least, they're gone.

Like a Toast

Two plates of prime rib;
shrimp cocktail;
French onion soup;
you're eighteen today.

I planned this night
for months, consulted
the guys at work,
sifted their advice:

—"Take him to the 'Vue"
(a strip club in Ypsi)
"Buy the kid a table dance,
something you both can enjoy."

—A cooler head suggested cigars,
a handful of thick Miduras—
perhaps your own humidor.
You'd probably keep computer discs in it.

—"My dad got me a gun,
a hunting rifle I've never fired.
It's still in the walnut case
under my bed with the dust bunnies."

Idiots! Snobs! Whoremongers! Enough!
None of them understood.
You and I converse far easier than any word
I ever shared with my father.

So tonight, when the dishes disappear

and I slide a wrapped box toward you,
it won't really matter what's inside.
Welcome, son, to the brotherhood of men.

basket

I would send all the Star Fruit of Heaven,
some strange prickly melon, with a thick rind
and a bitter-tangy fruit that sticks to the tongue
as well as every last persimmon in the place.

But the creamy pawpaw from last harvest are gone,
so we dug up the last treasures from the root cellar,
the seed corn we jarred up for next season,
and a fat envelope of pumpkin guts, dried, salted.

These provisions won't be enough, you know,
preparations hardly ever survive the first distress
of the journey. Sustenance must be scavenged,
roadside grasses, chewed as distraction, for comfort.

You'll find your diet hidden in bullrushes, amid dark woods.
Your life, its path and destination, requires special food.

Standing in the Kitchen, Talking about Danger

We herd our little loves with vague tales of strangers
and instill some sense of the unknown
and unexpected dangers
that may befall them. Even though we know
what some of those might be.
We tend our tongues and hope
edgy voices are enough
to make a vest of caution to clothe them in.

When we full well know,
when we can name harms
and places, dates and faces.

Time pleats like some accordion drape,
folds in on itself, and we are here two grown-ups.
I know what I must tell you,
but it's much more work to tell the truth.
The details can come out; we can uncover
what's been euphemized and edited:
who drowned, fled, bruised, lost, died.
Even with these histories, I would not have you full of cares,
but careful, walking not in shadow, but in light.

all yours

Another love might bury me;
when I'm not here, let go my heart.
But elemental love like ours
can see the worth of every part.

Another man might burn me up,
scattered remains signal I'm gone.
Commit my body to the sea,
simply dissolve and so move on.

I've been your treasure these long years;
I know you'd never let me be.
We are much more than dust and ash;
I ask you: make the most of me.

Some lack frugality or craft—
not handy with a plan or tool.
If nothing else, you are dextrous:
you'd know or find out what to do.

In this one-time undertaking
an honored partner known for thrift.
My molecules, materials;
my very self, a parting gift.

Phalanges made into jewelry.
Teeth sharpened to compose a blade.
Nails compounded into scrapers.
Artifacts anew to be made.

'Til Death

Old love might be recycled.
A femur as leg of a chair.
What once held me could support you.
Remembrance wreath woven from hair.

Eyes in a jar watch over you—
Superstition or modern art.
When my substance is not useful,
then let the compost do its part.

Nourish the soil with my atoms,
Plant seedlings we'd both adore.
Ev'n if I've made the most of life,
I ask you to make something more.

Agenda

After she's gone to the shop,
before you're expected at work,
you could do it. You could make it happen.
It wouldn't take long. It could all be over.

In the break room, between pointless requests,
you could unplug the computer,
knot a loop in the power cord.
Find something to support your weight.

Or you could just slip it over your head,
feel the relief, wicking away the stress.
Imagine floating, free at last. Free at last.
It wouldn't take long. It could all be over.

The awful wait, finished, this shrill masquerade.
It's not the suspense that's killing you.

Autopsy

The odds were against
this miscreant child:
two-headed, two-hearted,
doubled-chambers working at odds,

a mess of limbs,
tangled ambitions.
Not single-sighted Graeae,
but compounded,
ommatidia,

a pushmi-pullyu tugged
by divided intentions,
fur dirtied, seams stretched,
a struggle in loneliness.

A graft might repair
this natural blunder,
or one twin surrender unexpectedly
to save the other, only
to find existence impossible.

Taken apart,
stitched together
a mismatched patch.
An ongoing vivisection,
yet this living entity survives.

Nachlass

The widow uncovers a curio amid the wizard's chaos—
the wasted pages, dead pens and bent clips—
a simple white crystal, nearly clear. "Quartz?" she wonders.
Its angular geometry betrayed by artifice, wrapped in silver wire
like serpentine vertebrae encoiling a dragon's prize,
the stone nested like an egg, one smothered, dead.
A jeweler's hoard is hardly a nurturing brood.

"What a fool he was," she thinks, sweeping his papers in the bin
yet she cradles her palm around the strange artifact
so very much like a chunk of salt, the kind strewn
to clear treacherous paths, to melt cold barriers…
His last charm? She succumbs to whimsy, whispers a wish
then presses the piece to her tongue. She tastes only stone.
"Two fools," she thinks again. Grief is not magick;

The pendant performs no resurrection. Winter killed him.
Its cold spell broke his spirit, pronounced a chill sentence.
He laced his own neck, then waltzed on air, alone
leaving his messy remains, his dangling threads
for his discarded dance partner to tie up, to tidy.
His grimoires were dirtied with poetry addressed to her
but in the end his corpse chose a darker paramour.

In an eclipse of jealous anger, she pinches the odd brooch.
The precious metal lace snaps away, a worthless filigree
like romantic lines he'd once spun to encumber her heart.
Devotion is no demon, first summoned then encircled and possessed.
Love is more a cloudy stone, angular and unusual, only relatively pure
a hard murky gem, precious in daily use, yet oh so easily lost.
This revised fortune, she accepts and cherishes deep in her pocket.

a winter burial

you are dressed for the grave but not for digging them
so you're allowed to witness this grim worksite
no closer than the gravel ribbon edge. this field of pale dominoes,
where diesel equipment—dozer, claw, truck—
and workers with carharts, steam breath and steel-toed boots
scrabble the cold earth, excavate the casket space.
mourners, shoulder to shoulder, provide a wind fence. vain protection.

you refused to peer in his coffin, this Vietnam medic, this hero,
the nearest brother you had. no final bon mot accompanies him.
you struggle to speak, this brutal atmosphere turns any good words to
 waste heat.
entropy. knuckles ache, the stems of cut flowers steeped in ice water.
what justice, you wonder, what victory. a week earlier,
you'd strung a noose over your own head, cinched the knot tight,
hesitated atop a kitchen stool—tempted, contemplating, cowed
by that next step, that shallow fall to a similar place, a different vantage.

the slow machines settle the veteran's box deep beneath the frostline,
the first block of some hard foundation.
they grind to life then slink past the horizon.
full military honors. This is not about you.

Dressed in the Dark

The winter's cold has slowed us down.
Our liquid centers suffered a change of state.
We move unsynchronized, our clocks misset,
our actions mismatched as two dusty socks
fetched from deep under the bed.
If we looked in the mirror or at each other,
we might see the lines around our eyes,
we might question these clothes we've chosen.
You throw on your dark cloak these days,
the one that is far too large for you,
tripping your boots on the stairs,
hanging loose off your shoulders.
There's room enough for me to curl inside:
in the camouflage, we disappear.

Home Movies

You walk again!
You—almost a decade dead—
walk, as you used to, toes outward
in the peasant gait of our family's solid women.

You still turn your bad side away from the camera,
to hide your only flaw—a face half-paralyzed since birth:
empty ear; clear, unfocusing eye; mouth
that could only half smile.

I listened for your voice on the silent tape,
your feigned anger at grandchildren
in the old-world tongue you invented,
a language with no bad words.

How strange to see you walk again,
still more to dream of you walking.
In these dreams you turn to me
your perfect resurrected smile.

Ammonite

When we are gone, our bodies fossilized,
Our gaps filled by sparkle and stone,
Study this iridescence.
Cut in half by death, our mirroring,
our similarities exposed and preserved,
rough spots erased,
discord silenced.
Our spiral chambers polished
reveal soft interiors,
vulnerable predatory affection,
collected in a chambered shell.
When we lie extinct like the dinosaurs,
study this love that swam
through catastrophic seas and
warm shallow waters with the same ease,
note the imperfections,
both hidden and magnified,
our stubbornly attached
illusion of symmetry.

Hunted

a nightmare

I wander outdoors, past my sleeping loves,
to survey the wind and clouds
the screen creaks open
as a broom stick falls
to block the way back
everything unhinges
danger waiting
a huge dog,
dark fur
eyes bright red
darker than night
His white points erupt,
a snarl runs down his back,
puffed-up menace growls and snaps
I am the door.
I am the wall between teeth and skin.
Eyes locked, a staring contest.
The dog deciding
I am
still
afraid

In a blink, he's gone and I move

Second Sight

An unseasonable morning fog blackens the pavement,
the two-lane hospital road transformed to treacherous ice.

Landmarks a block distant erased from memory.
A car length ahead, even a red pickup skids, indistinct.

Another dread appointment prompts our slow parade,
rounds of more tests, puzzles, symptoms, mysteries.

A rude passenger with sharp elbows crowds our hearts.
A dull ache pulsing high in our torso—probably benign.

===

Cold snapped the afternoon into hard focus. A snowy vista
surrounds the parking structure, reveals its bitter majesty.

Chain links encased in crystallized mist now frame
a valley of crosshatched branches, each a tight precise stroke.

Worry—a long held breath coaxed to cautious release—
becomes a cottony wisp, dissipated by a temporary wind.

We will not long survive this brutal season, this severe passage
this difficult transition. We travel praying never to arrive.

Twice Eurydice

When blood first arced from my vein,
advanced beginners convinced me not to flee
with promises of happy smiles, good results.
The needle slid in on second try

and guided me to that underworld,
that gauzy prison, that dreamy maze.
I paid for my escape with a quart of tears,
and three teeth, cut from bone.

My gratitude flowed uncontrolled though
my jaw was swollen for a full week.

My second trip, the second time
that I slipped under, we'd slipped up.

Love knows few limits—
maybe sleep, patience, will-power—
and two were plenty to fill our arms
so we incised that decision in his loins.

The snip alas was made too late.
The bloom of summer
forced us to decide again,
this time written on my flesh.

I swore violins swelled as a circle
of witnesses gathered to watch over me.
Blankets bound my arms like warm waves
where I swam, an unseasonable fish.

When I came up for air, fog-bound,
bloated with senseless questions,
my Orpheus brought me home
and together we mourned that long day.

My second ransom left safe below,
a shiny pebble slipped to the ocean's floor.
I purchased my return with a sacrificed idea,
an adventure averted, a dream I let go.

The Snow-bike

When your age was mine,

    summer was cold as winter's now.

We were so poor we built our bikes

    from chains and scraps of old snow

left from the Ice factory down the block.

    It was cold work then to make fun.

We spit and packed, used icicles for spokes

    and still it wobbled if left in the sun.

The Ghost Who Didn't Follow Me Home

Oh Dead Papa, I try to picture you
perched on wedding cake clouds at peace,
a beloved patriarch on a painted wall
perhaps impatient, lonesome for your bride,

But I recognized you in a February breeze
haunting the aisles of the discount store, a desire
aching for bargains and justification, eager to
prove the worth of your soul by the pennies you save.

You approved of my purchases—economy sizes
and store brands. But I sensed the company of demons
who tricked you to squander your weekends and dark evenings
scavenging coupons and scoping out sales.

"Oh Papa, you're homeless and beggar-desperate.
You own no house to clutter with sale-priced loot
to clog like the arteries that murdered you.
Come home with me," I lured… then lost your ghost.

But I was never the product, the deal you sought.

Rocket Man

Fatherhood will rip a man apart,
test his components, scatter his baggage wide.
Worse than sabotage, its burst explodes
the sleek trajectory of boyhood dreams.

Domestic terror sucks the comfort from habits,
sudden as cabin pressure lost to space.
Hold your breath. Traverse this void by instinct,
not instruments, their dials, cracked, corrupt.

Stress will finally shatter your hull,
strew your ruins beyond any vain horizon,
a wreckage field broader than any airport,
acres of destination, all wide of the mark.

No reunion can re-assemble this crashed man;
No ransom need redeem this blessed hijack.

Apocalypse

If the world winks out in our lifetimes,
let it fall on a day when we can speak a civil word.
We might rise rested from a shared bed, our growls
hibernating, voices affection-softened.
Let us have put our arguments outside
like a line of empty milk bottles,
the constant hurts, claws retracted, blood-free.
Rain, snow, sleet—doesn't matter,
but let it be a day when we are friends.
The sky can be clouded;
singing birds are not necessary.
The traffic can rush or jam as it wills.
Leaves can bloom or fall.
Let's not be finicky,
if it's really the End.

If requests are allowed,
then this:
a plate with crumbs
from a pastry we just shared,
two cups of coffee still hot,
we laugh
over remembering the trip out west—
   singing "wimoweh" together
    with the children strapped in the back
    as the Canadian prairies and sky
    unfolded like a bolt of fabric
    spreading beige and purple and blue—
or marvel
about a new memory one tells the other,
   a story not yet shared

   but fresh as cotton candy.

Before the lights go out,
before fire or bang or the shake of catastrophe,
the exchange of recognition,
a slow nod that says I knew you,
spreading across our faces,
as roiling, powerful, and distinctive
as a mushroom cloud.

Ostara

They've stood guard, patiently,
around us, over us, overlooked,
for years, the maple trees
larger than the span of our arms.

In late winter, shit-colored snow
still underfoot, soil hard, brown-tufted,
we probe through their ancient bark,
hammer spile, collect heart-blood.

For weeks we follow the slow drip,
gather their clear fluid in gallon jugs
then place our largest, strongest pot
over the flames to begin the rite.

The numbers are hard, daunting.
24 hours of simmering steam;
40 gallons of sap yielding
a single pitcher of precious syrup.

The first day uncoils easily.
We tend the fire, feed twigs
we've dried all winter, nearly
dancing around the flames.

Tending demands slight attention,
so we trouble the beds, rake away
the last tired scrabble of mulch.
Only the weeds have roused.

We produce our own clouds,

sheets of white fluff rippling
from the rim. But we bore soon.
Even this alchemy becomes rote.

Errands draw us in turn, while one
stays vigilant. The danger not conflagration,
rather the flame's tender curls
would expire without constant fuel. The liquor freeze.

Late afternoon, clouds sprinkle
the proceedings, wet the ground.
We stand, lid held like a shield
protecting our pot, stirring its gold.

The sky clears come evening,
birds converse in the trees then silence,
just the meditative splash of paddle,
the contemplative roar of embers.

The world changes around us,
settles into patterns of darkness.
In these shadows, we are overlooked.
We stand like trees, quiet, at peace.

We risk a sample of this sweet smoke.
We joke, nearly giddy. "At this rate it'll be
ready for pancakes after Sunrise Service"
if we still rose to mark the Resurrection.

After midnight, we transfer this elixir
to a smaller pot, drag it indoors
to finish over our kitchen stove.
The home stretch now, the final boil.

We fret less, nod off while monitoring
the pot, now as mundane as broth,

the spectacle of wood flame exchanged
for domestic dial controls, predictable blue jets.

We wake amid clouds, the sting
of burnt sugar rasping our noses.
While we dozed, blissful, so sure, so content,
our bounty scorched. We ruined both sap and pan.

We'd come so close, nearly made home sweet,
yet during the watch that ends the night,
we'd betrayed our goal, like apostles asleep
while their Saviour prayed at Gethsemane.

Samhain

The princess and her vagabond brother race to the door,
yell breathlessly, collect their treasure in pillow cases
then leap the stairs and cut a course through the leafy yard
to the neighbor's lighted porch, the next Halloween house.

The gray lady slowly appears, hunched but regal,
works her eyes to recognize her impatient guests.
She appreciates every detail of their improvised disguises.
Once rewarded, they rush away, wisps disappearing in the dark.

The thin walls between generations dissolve tonight,
an instant long enough for blessings to pass across the threshold.
Soon, pillows will be weighed down with tired heads;
soon—too soon—the porch light will shut off.

Cold Solstice

We greet this long night cautiously,
an ordeal, yet another holiday trial
for our poorly yoked temperaments,
my horned mask, your impromptu disguise.

We mull near the walls, admire their decoration,
the strings of gathered trash, painted gold
woven with tinsel. Ruined ourselves, we feel
at home amid this glorious, gathered wreckage.

The rhythm irresistibly mixes with our pretense.
None here are precisely who they seem. Together,
we move, generate sweat, radiant heat,
that sweet writhing alchemy of becoming.

Naughty fauns and foul nymphs cavort,
their grinding and wiggling rewarded
with periodic whipping by attendant trolls,
a scourge that encourages their frenzy.

From the ornate stage, a cast of marionettes
observes, mimics, mocks our rictus, the ritual
death throes of another year's disappointments.
    "What fools these be, who pretend to be mortal…"

When the speakers die at midnight,
when the hard brass, the speaking wind
of trumpet and tuba, trombone and drum
begin a new song. We are ready.

We follow this fresh appeal outside,
and assemble, half-transformed,
around fire torches, line frozen city streets,
eager for this annual lost parade.

For our standard, our flag of allegiance,
we stretch a bloody sheet
where we project shadow-puppets,
monstrous flickering outlines of glee and woe.

Past every bar, across the chilly black river,
forsaking all domesticated festivities,
through scrub and bracken, we follow
until we halt, cold, dark, expectant.

The prepared barrels won't catch
so we empty our wallets for tinder—
receipts, phone numbers, business cards.
We sacrifice our regrets to kindle these flames.

We are not the first on this tribal field.
Jagged constructions jut up in the dark,
assemblages of wood and glass, wire and plastic,
like homes for the restless spirits who infiltrate our revels.

A thousand times I lose you in this frigid crowd,
forget your temporary face, drift in the tattered dark,
distracted by the spark from a kindred eye,
the gentle warmth of a knowing smile.

Until the magnet of your gaze recollects me
and face claps to face, our roles conform again.
Reconfirmed, we clasp hands and hold fast.
Another magic supersedes this masquerade.

Night is no less dark. The cold still bitter.
The coming seasons will recycle tired scripts;
we will torture each other by will and accident
no doubt, but we depart this crucible partners.

About the Authors

James Frederick Leach writes darkly speculative poetry, fiction & drama and is a contributing editor to the website / Youtube channel dailynightmare.com which celebrates Midwest Highbrow Horror. Jim's poetry has been nominated for the Elgin award and his play about John the Baptist won the CITA national playwriting award. A Gemini with Gemini rising, Jim is fascinated by the magical power of words from the sounds and rhythms they make when spoken to the shapes and patterns of letter forms when written. In his spare time, Jim makes masks, reads tarot and paints dead things.

Janice Leach bakes pies with local ingredients; volunteers at a long term garden project in youth detention; loves and defends those around her; and writes about it all in poems, grants, and blogs. As an undergraduate at the University of Michigan, she received a Hopwood Award for poetry. She tends a rollicking kitchen garden filled with heirloom vegetables and fruit trees. Her future plans include more life, more love, more magic, and more poetry.

Jim and Janice grew up less than 2 miles apart in Dearborn, Michigan, the birthplace of Henry Ford and the Assembly Line. They fell in love at church youth group, and keeping track of them immediately became the nightmare of the youth director. During their three and a half decades together, the pair have published four volumes of Quick Shivers from Dailynightmare.com, and blogs including the Dailynightmare.com and 20minutegarden.com. They have been blessed with a fabulous daughter, a fantastic son, a funky cool daughter-in-law and a wonderful granddaughter. They grow tomatoes near a 100-year old lilac, listen for ghosts in the midnight, and get up early to discuss each other's dreams. They are currently busy with various schemes botanical, physical, and metaphysical as well as another collection of collaboratively written poetry.

CPSIA information can be obtained
at www.ICGtesting.com
Printed in the USA
FFOW04n2111220117
31609FF